Project 2025 Blueprint

Charting the path to a brighter future. Innovative strategies for a sustainable tomorrow.

Emmanuel Smith

Table of Contents

The "Project 2025 Blueprint" represents a comprehensive and visionary plan to reshape the trajectory of our nation by the year 2025. Rooted in a steadfast commitment to progress and equity, this ambitious blueprint outlines a strategic roadmap that boldly addresses the most pressing challenges of our time.

From revitalizing our economic foundations to championing environmental sustainability and fostering greater social inclusion, this project harnesses the collective power of innovative policies, strategic public-private collaborations, and transformative technological advancements. By aligning our collective resources and expertise, we are poised to usher in a new era of shared prosperity, resilience, and opportunity for all.

At the heart of this blueprint lies a profound recognition that the status quo is no longer sufficient to meet the evolving needs of our rapidly changing world. Demographic shifts, technological disruptions, and widening socioeconomic disparities have exposed the cracks in our current systems, underscoring the urgent imperative for comprehensive, multi-faceted solutions. Project 2025 represents a bold and visionary response to these pressing realities, grounded in a steadfast belief that by working together, we can shape a future that is more equitable, sustainable, and prosperous for generations to come.

This introduction sets the stage for the detailed objectives, implementation strategies, and timelines that will guide us towards realizing the transformative potential of Project 2025. Through a strategic blend of policy initiatives, public-private collaborations, and technological innovations, we will forge a path forward that prioritizes the wellbeing of our citizens, the resilience of our communities, and the stewardship of our shared environment. By aligning our collective efforts and resources, we are poised to catalyze positive change across all sectors of society, ultimately building a future that serves the best interests of our nation and the global community.

CHAPTER ONE

Key Objectives

The "Project 2025 Blueprint" outlines three overarching and interconnected objectives that will guide our collective efforts towards a brighter future:

1. Economic Transformation:
At the forefront of our vision is the revitalization of our national economy, driven by a comprehensive strategy to foster innovation, enhance productivity, and create sustainable employment opportunities. This objective entails modernizing our industrial sectors, investing in emerging technologies, and nurturing a thriving entrepreneurial ecosystem. By diversifying our economic base, we aim to build resilience against market fluctuations and position our

nation as a global leader in high-value industries.

2. Environmental Sustainability:

Recognizing the urgent need to address the pressing challenges of climate change and environmental degradation, Project 2025 places a strong emphasis on promoting sustainable practices across all sectors. This includes transitioning to renewable energy sources, implementing robust waste management systems, and incentivizing the development of eco-friendly technologies. Through targeted policy initiatives and public-private collaborations, we will work to conserve our natural resources, protect biodiversity, and mitigate the long-term impacts of human activity on our planet.

3. Social Equity:

Underpinning our vision for a brighter future is a steadfast commitment to fostering greater social equity and inclusion. This objective aims to address longstanding disparities in access to quality education, healthcare, and economic opportunities, empowering marginalized communities and ensuring that the benefits of progress are equitably distributed. By investing in targeted social programs, strengthening social safety nets, and promoting diversity and representation, we will work to create a more just and inclusive society that offers equal opportunities for all.

These three key objectives are inextricably linked, forming a holistic and interdependent framework that will guide the implementation of Project 2025. By aligning our efforts across these critical domains, we will lay the foundation for a sustainable, prosperous, and equitable future that serves the best interests of our nation and its people.

1.1. Economic Transformation

At the forefront of the "Project 2025 Blueprint" is the revitalization of our national economy, driven by a comprehensive strategy to foster innovation, enhance productivity, and create sustainable employment opportunities. This objective recognizes the need to modernize our industrial sectors, invest in emerging technologies, and nurture a thriving entrepreneurial ecosystem.

By diversifying our economic base, we aim to build resilience against market fluctuations and position our nation as a global leader in high-value industries. This will involve targeted investments in cutting-edge research and development, supporting the growth of small and medium-sized enterprises, and implementing policies that incentivize the adoption of advanced manufacturing techniques and digital technologies.

Through strategic public-private partnerships, we will leverage the expertise and resources of the business community to catalyze economic transformation. This collaborative approach will enable us to identify and address bottlenecks, streamline regulatory frameworks, and foster an environment that is conducive to innovation and risk-taking.

Integral to this economic transformation is the prioritization of sustainable and inclusive growth. We will work to ensure that the benefits of progress are equitably distributed, creating pathways for marginalized communities to actively participate in and contribute to the economic prosperity of our nation. By aligning our efforts across these critical areas, we will lay the foundation for a dynamic, resilient, and future-oriented economy that serves the best interests of our citizens and enhances our global competitiveness.

At the core of the "Project 2025 Blueprint" is a bold and comprehensive strategy to revitalize our national economy, positioning our country as a global leader in innovation, productivity, and sustainable growth. This economic transformation objective recognizes the urgent need to modernize our industrial sectors, harness the power of emerging technologies, and foster a thriving entrepreneurial ecosystem.

Central to this vision is the diversification of our economic base, which will enable us to build resilience against market fluctuations and capitalize on the opportunities presented by rapidly evolving industries and consumer demands. This multi-faceted approach will involve strategic investments in cutting-edge research and development, targeted support for small and medium-sized enterprises, and the implementation of policies that incentivize the adoption of advanced manufacturing techniques and digital technologies.

Through strategic public-private partnerships, we will leverage the expertise, resources, and innovative capacity of the business community to catalyze this economic transformation. By fostering close collaboration between the public and private sectors, we will be able to identify and address key bottlenecks, streamline regulatory frameworks, and create an environment that is conducive to risk-taking and entrepreneurial activity.

Integral to this vision is the prioritization of sustainable and inclusive growth, ensuring that the benefits of economic progress are equitably distributed across all segments of our society. We will work to create pathways for marginalized communities to actively participate in and contribute to the prosperity of our nation, empowering them with the skills, resources, and opportunities necessary to thrive in the evolving economic landscape.

By aligning our efforts across these critical areas, we will lay the foundation for a dynamic, resilient, and future-oriented economy that not only enhances our global competitiveness but also improves the overall quality of life for our citizens. Through targeted investments, strategic partnerships, and innovative policy solutions, we will transform our economic landscape, positioning our nation as a trailblazer in the new era of sustainable and inclusive prosperity.

1.2. Environmental Sustainability

Recognizing the urgent need to address the pressing challenges of climate change and environmental degradation, the "Project 2025 Blueprint" places a strong emphasis on promoting sustainable practices across all sectors of our economy and society. This objective is grounded in the fundamental belief that long-term prosperity and well-being are inextricably linked to the health and resilience of our natural ecosystems.

At the heart of this environmental sustainability pillar is a comprehensive strategy to transition our energy infrastructure towards renewable and clean energy sources. This will involve the large-scale deployment of solar, wind, and other clean energy technologies, coupled with investments in grid modernization and energy storage solutions. By reducing our reliance on fossil fuels, we will not only mitigate greenhouse gas emissions but also create new economic opportunities in the burgeoning green energy sector.

Complementing our energy transition efforts, the "Project 2025 Blueprint" also prioritizes the implementation of robust waste management systems and the promotion of circular economy principles. This will entail the development of innovative recycling and upcycling initiatives, as well as the incentivization of sustainable product design and manufacturing practices. By minimizing waste and promoting the reuse and repurposing of materials, we will work to conserve natural resources and reduce the environmental impact of our economic activities.

Moreover, the environmental sustainability objective emphasizes the critical importance of protecting and restoring our natural habitats, biodiversity, and ecological systems. Through targeted conservation efforts, strategic land-use planning, and the promotion of sustainable agriculture and forestry practices, we will strive to safeguard the delicate balance of our planet's ecosystems, ensuring that future generations can continue to benefit from the invaluable services they provide.

By aligning our collective efforts across these key areas, the "Project 2025 Blueprint" aims to position our nation as a global leader in environmental stewardship, driving sustainable innovation and inspiring others to join us in our quest for a more resilient and ecologically balanced future.

1.3. Social Equity

At the heart of the "Project 2025 Blueprint" is a steadfast commitment to fostering greater social equity and inclusion, recognizing that the long-term prosperity and resilience of our nation is inextricably linked to the well-being and empowerment of all our citizens.

This objective is rooted in the acknowledgment of longstanding disparities in access to quality education, healthcare, and economic opportunities, which have disproportionately impacted marginalized communities. By addressing these systemic inequities, we aim to create a more just and equitable society that offers equal pathways to success and fulfillment, regardless of one's background or socioeconomic status.

Central to this vision is the strategic investment in targeted social programs and initiatives that empower individuals and communities. This will include the expansion of affordable housing options, the enhancement of public healthcare infrastructure, and the improvement of educational outcomes in underserved areas. Through these concerted efforts, we will work to uplift the most vulnerable members of our society, providing them with the resources, skills, and opportunities necessary to thrive and contribute to the overall progress of our nation.

Complementing these direct interventions, the "Project 2025 Blueprint" also emphasizes the need to promote diversity, representation, and inclusivity across all sectors of our society. This will involve the implementation of policies and practices that foster an environment of respect, understanding, and equal opportunity, ensuring that the decision-making processes and leadership structures within our public and private institutions are reflective of the diverse tapestry of our population.

By addressing the root causes of social inequity and actively dismantling the barriers that have hindered the full participation and advancement of marginalized groups, we will work to create a more cohesive and inclusive society. This holistic approach to social equity will not only uplift individual lives but also strengthen the fabric of our communities, ultimately contributing to the long-term prosperity and stability of our nation.

CHAPTER TWO

Implementation Strategies

At the forefront of our implementation approach are targeted policy initiatives that will create the enabling environment for the realization of our key objectives. This will involve the enactment of legislation, the establishment of regulatory frameworks, and the deployment of fiscal and monetary incentives to drive progress across the economic, environmental, and social domains.

For example, in support of our economic transformation objective, we will work to implement tax credits and investment schemes that encourage businesses to invest in research and development, adopt advanced manufacturing technologies, and expand sustainable production methods. Similarly, we will introduce policies that mandate the transition to renewable energy sources, promote sustainable waste management practices, and incentivize the conservation and restoration of natural habitats.

Complementing these economic and environmental policies, we will also champion social equity-focused initiatives, such as increased funding for public education, universal healthcare coverage, and targeted programs that address the unique challenges faced by marginalized communities.

Public-Private Partnerships
Recognizing that the ambitious goals of Project 2025 cannot be achieved through government action alone, our implementation strategy will place a strong emphasis on forging strategic public-private partnerships. By leveraging the expertise, resources, and

innovative capacity of the business community, we will be able to develop and scale solutions that address the complex challenges we face.

These collaborations will take various forms, from joint research and development initiatives to the co-creation of sustainable business models and the co-design of targeted social programs. By aligning the interests and efforts of the public and private sectors, we will unlock synergies, streamline processes, and ensure that the benefits of our transformative efforts are widely distributed.

Technological Advancements
Underpinning the successful implementation of the "Project 2025 Blueprint" will be the strategic integration of emerging technologies and digital solutions. From automation and artificial intelligence to renewable energy systems and smart

infrastructure, we will harness the power of technological innovation to drive efficiency, enhance productivity, and enable the scalable deployment of our sustainability and equity initiatives.

By investing in the research, development, and deployment of cutting-edge technologies, we will not only address pressing challenges but also position our nation as a global leader in innovation. This technological foundation will be crucial in catalyzing the systemic changes required to achieve our ambitious goals and create a brighter, more sustainable future for all.

Through the coordinated and strategic deployment of these three core implementation strategies, the "Project 2025 Blueprint" will translate its transformative vision into tangible, measurable, and sustainable progress, positioning our nation as a beacon of progress and prosperity in the 21st century.

2.1. Policy Initiatives

Policy Initiatives

At the heart of the "Project 2025 Blueprint's" implementation strategy lies a comprehensive suite of policy initiatives designed to create the enabling environment for the realization of its key objectives. These targeted policy interventions will span the economic, environmental, and social domains, working in tandem to drive transformative change across our nation.

Economic Policy Initiatives
In support of our economic transformation objective, we will introduce a range of policies aimed at

incentivizing innovation, enhancing productivity, and fostering the growth of sustainable industries. This will include the implementation of tax credits and investment schemes that encourage businesses to invest in research and development, adopt advanced manufacturing technologies, and expand their sustainable production capabilities.

Additionally, we will work to streamline regulatory frameworks, eliminate bureaucratic bottlenecks, and provide targeted support for small and medium-sized enterprises. By creating an ecosystem that is conducive to entrepreneurial activity and risk-taking, we will cultivate a thriving, diversified, and future-oriented economy.

Environmental Policy Initiatives
Recognizing the urgent need to address the challenges of climate change and environmental degradation, the "Project

2025 Blueprint" will prioritize the enactment of bold policy initiatives that drive the transition towards renewable energy sources and sustainable resource management.

This will include the establishment of mandatory renewable energy targets, the implementation of carbon pricing mechanisms, and the introduction of incentives for the adoption of energy-efficient technologies and sustainable practices. We will also champion policies that promote the circular economy, such as extended producer responsibility schemes and robust waste management regulations.

Moreover, we will develop comprehensive land-use planning policies and strengthen conservation efforts to protect and restore our natural habitats, biodiversity, and ecological systems, ensuring the long-term resilience of our shared environment.

Social Equity Policy Initiatives
Underpinning the "Project 2025 Blueprint" is a steadfast commitment to fostering greater social equity and inclusion. To this end, we will champion a suite of policy initiatives aimed at addressing the root causes of systemic disparities and empowering marginalized communities.

This will involve increased funding for public education, the expansion of affordable housing options, and the enhancement of universal healthcare coverage. We will also introduce policies that promote diversity and representation in our institutions, ensure fair and equal employment opportunities, and provide targeted support for vulnerable populations.

By aligning these economic, environmental, and social policy initiatives, the "Project 2025 Blueprint" will create an integrated and holistic framework for change, laying the groundwork for the successful implementation of its transformative vision.

2.2. Public-Private Partnerships

Recognizing that the ambitious goals of the "Project 2025 Blueprint" cannot be achieved through government action alone, the implementation strategy places a strong emphasis on forging strategic public-private partnerships. By leveraging the expertise, resources, and innovative capacity of the business community, we will be able to develop and scale solutions that address the complex challenges we face.

These collaborations will take various forms, from joint research and development initiatives to the co-creation of sustainable business models and the co-design of targeted social programs. By aligning the interests and efforts of the public and private sectors, we will unlock synergies, streamline processes, and ensure that the benefits of our transformative efforts are widely distributed.

One key area of focus for these public-private partnerships will be the economic transformation objective. We will work closely with industry leaders to identify barriers to growth and innovation, subsequently designing and implementing policies that incentivize businesses to invest in emerging technologies, adopt sustainable practices, and expand their operations in a manner that promotes long-term prosperity.

This collaborative approach will also be central to our environmental sustainability initiatives. By partnering with corporate leaders, we will develop innovative solutions for renewable energy generation, waste management, and ecological restoration. Together, we will devise business models that seamlessly integrate environmental stewardship with economic growth, driving the creation of a thriving green economy.

In the realm of social equity, public-private partnerships will be instrumental in the design and delivery of targeted programs that address the unique challenges faced by marginalized communities. Through joint efforts, we will leverage the insights, resources, and networks of the private sector to enhance access to quality education, healthcare, and economic opportunities, empowering individuals and families to overcome systemic barriers and actively participate in the progress of our nation.

By fostering these strategic alliances, the "Project 2025 Blueprint" will harness the collective strength and ingenuity of the public and private sectors, unlocking synergies that transcend traditional boundaries and paving the way for transformative, scalable, and sustainable solutions. This collaborative approach will be a key driver in the successful implementation of our ambitious vision for the future. At the core of the "Project 2025 Blueprint's" implementation strategy is a steadfast commitment to forging strategic and multi-faceted public-private partnerships. Recognizing that the scale and complexity of the challenges we face cannot be addressed by the government alone, this collaborative approach aims to leverage the expertise, resources, and innovative capacity of the business community to develop and scale impactful solutions.

These partnerships will take on a variety of forms, each tailored to the unique requirements of the initiatives being undertaken. In the realm of economic transformation, for example, we will work closely with industry leaders to identify key barriers to growth and innovation. Through joint task forces and roundtable discussions, we will design and implement policies that provide clear incentives for businesses to invest in emerging technologies, adopt sustainable production methods, and expand their operations in a manner that promotes long-term prosperity and resilience.

Similarly, in the pursuit of environmental sustainability, public-private collaborations will be instrumental in the development and deployment of innovative solutions for renewable energy generation, waste management, and ecological restoration. By aligning the interests and capabilities of the public and private sectors, we will devise business models that seamlessly integrate environmental stewardship with economic growth, catalyzing the creation of a thriving green economy.

The realm of social equity will also see the transformative impact of these strategic partnerships. By leveraging the insights, resources, and networks of the private sector, we will co-design and co-deliver targeted programs that address the unique challenges faced by marginalized communities. This collaborative approach will enhance access to quality education, healthcare, and economic opportunities, empowering individuals and families to overcome systemic barriers and actively participate in the progress of our nation.

Underpinning the success of these public-private partnerships will be a commitment to transparency, accountability, and equitable risk-sharing. We will establish clear governance structures and performance metrics to ensure that the interests of all stakeholders are aligned and that the benefits of our collaborative efforts are widely distributed.

Through these strategic alliances, the "Project 2025 Blueprint" will harness the collective strength and ingenuity of the public and private sectors, unlocking synergies that transcend traditional boundaries and paving the way for transformative, scalable, and sustainable solutions. This collaborative approach will be a key driver in the successful implementation of our ambitious vision for the future, positioning our nation as a global leader in innovative, equitable, and environmentally-conscious progress.

2.3. Technological Advancements

Underpinning the successful implementation of the "Project 2025 Blueprint" will be the strategic integration of emerging technologies and digital solutions. From automation and artificial intelligence to renewable energy systems and smart infrastructure, we will harness the power of technological innovation to drive efficiency, enhance productivity, and enable the scalable deployment of our sustainability and equity initiatives.

At the forefront of our technological advancements will be the deployment of cutting-edge automation and artificial intelligence (AI) systems. By automating repetitive and labor-intensive tasks, we will unlock new efficiencies across a wide range of industries, freeing up human resources to focus on more complex, value-adding activities. Furthermore, the integration of AI-powered decision-making and predictive analytics will enable us to optimize resource allocation, streamline operations, and enhance the overall productivity of our economic systems.

In the realm of sustainability, we will make significant investments in the research, development, and deployment of renewable energy technologies. This will include the large-scale installation of solar, wind, and next-generation energy storage systems, as well as the development of smart grid infrastructure to facilitate the integration of these clean energy sources. By leveraging the rapid advancements in renewable energy technologies, we will accelerate our transition away from fossil fuels, reducing our carbon footprint and enhancing the long-term resilience of our energy supply.

Complementing our energy transformation efforts, we will also harness the power of digital technologies to drive innovation in waste management and resource efficiency. Through the deployment of Internet of Things (IoT) sensors, blockchain-enabled traceability systems, and advanced material science, we will optimize waste collection and recycling processes, promote the circular economy, and minimize the environmental impact of our production and consumption patterns.

Beyond the economic and environmental domains, technological advancements will also play a crucial role in addressing social equity challenges. By leveraging digital platforms, mobile applications, and cloud-based services, we will enhance the accessibility and delivery of critical social services, such as healthcare, education, and financial inclusion. These technological solutions will empower marginalized communities, providing them with the tools and resources necessary to overcome systemic barriers and actively participate in the progress of our nation.

By investing in the research, development, and deployment of cutting-edge technologies, the "Project 2025 Blueprint" will not only address pressing challenges but also position our nation as a global leader in innovation. This technological foundation will be crucial in catalyzing the systemic changes required to achieve our ambitious goals and create a brighter, more sustainable future for all.

CHAPTER THREE

Timeline and Milestones

This timeline has been carefully crafted to ensure that our efforts are both ambitious and achievable, with a steadfast focus on delivering tangible results within the next five years. By establishing a clear roadmap and tracking our progress through well-defined milestones, we will maintain momentum, foster accountability, and adapt our strategies as necessary to overcome any unforeseen challenges.

In the near-term, our immediate priorities will center around the laying of a strong foundational framework. This will involve the enactment of the necessary policy initiatives, the establishment of public-private partnerships, and the initial deployment of technological solutions to jumpstart our economic, environmental, and social equity initiatives.

By the end of 2023, we aim to have the majority of our policy frameworks in place, with clear targets and implementation plans for each of our key objectives. This will include the introduction of renewable energy mandates, the implementation of sustainable procurement policies, and the launch of targeted social programs to address disparities in education, healthcare, and economic opportunities.

As we move into 2024, our focus will shift towards the scaling and optimization of these initiatives. We will work to refine our policies, strengthen our public-private collaborations, and leverage emerging technologies to drive greater impact and efficiency. This phase will see the large-scale rollout of renewable energy projects, the expansion of circular economy initiatives, and the enhancement of social safety nets to reach more communities in need.

By the culmination of Project 2025, we expect to have achieved significant and measurable progress across all three of our key objectives. This will include the attainment of our renewable energy targets, the reduction of our carbon footprint and waste generation, and the demonstrable improvement in key social equity indicators, such as educational attainment, healthcare access, and employment rates.

Importantly, the timeline and milestones outlined in this blueprint are not static, but rather a living framework that will be continuously evaluated and adjusted as necessary. We recognize that the challenges we face are complex and ever-evolving, and as such, we are committed to maintaining a nimble and adaptive approach that allows us to capitalize on new opportunities and respond to emerging threats.

By adhering to this comprehensive timeline and tracking our progress through the achievement of key milestones, the "Project 2025 Blueprint" will ensure that our ambitious vision for the future remains on track, driving transformative change and setting our nation on a path towards a more prosperous, equitable, and sustainable tomorrow. This strategic roadmap has been carefully designed to balance ambition and achievability, ensuring that we maintain momentum, foster accountability, and adapt our strategies as necessary to overcome any unforeseen challenges.

Near-Term Priorities (2023-2024)

In the immediate future, our primary focus will be on laying a strong foundational framework for the successful execution of the project's key objectives. This will involve the enactment of the necessary policy initiatives, the establishment of public-private partnerships, and the initial deployment of technological solutions to jumpstart our economic, environmental, and social equity efforts.

By the end of 2023, we aim to have the majority of our policy frameworks in place, with clear targets and implementation plans for each of our priority areas. This will include the introduction of renewable energy mandates, the implementation of sustainable procurement policies, and the launch of targeted social programs to address disparities in education, healthcare, and economic opportunities.

As we move into 2024, our focus will shift towards the scaling and optimization of these initiatives. We will work to refine our policies, strengthen our public-private collaborations, and leverage emerging technologies to drive greater impact and efficiency. This phase will see the large-scale rollout of renewable energy projects, the expansion of circular economy initiatives, and the enhancement of social safety nets to reach more communities in need.

Achieving Transformative Change (2025)
By the culmination of Project 2025, we expect to have achieved significant and measurable progress across all three of our key objectives. This will include the attainment of our renewable energy targets, the reduction of our carbon footprint and waste generation, and the demonstrable improvement in key social equity indicators, such as educational

attainment, healthcare access, and employment rates.

Importantly, the timeline and milestones outlined in this blueprint are not static, but rather a living framework that will be continuously evaluated and adjusted as necessary. We recognize that the challenges we face are complex and ever-evolving, and as such, we are committed to maintaining a nimble and adaptive approach that allows us to capitalize on new opportunities and respond to emerging threats.

Through this comprehensive timeline and the achievement of well-defined milestones, the "Project 2025 Blueprint" will ensure that our ambitious vision for the future remains on track, driving transformative change and setting our nation on a path towards a more prosperous, equitable, and sustainable tomorrow. By adhering to this strategic roadmap, we will be able to hold ourselves accountable, celebrate our successes, and make the necessary course corrections to fulfill the promise of a brighter future for all.

The "Project 2025 Blueprint" represents a bold and comprehensive plan to reshape the trajectory of our nation, positioning us as a global leader in sustainable economic growth, environmental stewardship, and social equity. This ambitious vision is underpinned by a meticulously crafted implementation strategy that leverages the power of policy initiatives, public-private partnerships, and technological advancements to drive transformative change across all sectors of our society.

At the heart of this blueprint lies a steadfast commitment to economic transformation, recognizing the urgent need to modernize our industrial base, foster innovation, and create sustainable employment opportunities for all. By diversifying our economic landscape and harnessing the potential of emerging technologies, we will build resilience, enhance productivity, and solidify our position as a competitive force in the global marketplace.

Complementing our economic objectives is an unwavering focus on environmental sustainability, which will guide us towards a future where prosperity and ecological harmony coexist in perfect balance. Through the large-scale deployment of renewable energy solutions, the implementation of robust waste management systems, and the preservation of our natural habitats, we will work to mitigate the devastating impacts of climate change and safeguard the delicate balance of our planet's ecosystems for generations to come.

Underpinning these economic and environmental transformations is a steadfast commitment to social equity, which aims to address longstanding disparities in access to quality education, healthcare, and economic opportunities. By empowering marginalized communities, promoting diversity and inclusivity, and investing in targeted social programs, we will create a more just and cohesive society that offers equal pathways to success and fulfillment for all.

As we embark on this transformative journey, we recognize that the challenges we face are complex and multifaceted. However, by aligning our collective efforts, leveraging strategic partnerships, and harnessing the power of technological innovation, we are confident in our ability to turn this ambitious vision into a tangible reality. The economic transformation pillar focuses on modernizing our industries, fostering innovation, and creating sustainable jobs. By diversifying our economy and leveraging emerging technologies, we aim to enhance our global competitiveness while ensuring equitable prosperity for all.

Parallel to this is a steadfast focus on environmental sustainability. Through large-scale renewable energy deployment, robust waste management, and habitat conservation, we will work to mitigate climate change and maintain the delicate balance of our ecosystems.

Underpinning these economic and environmental goals is a resolute dedication to social equity. By empowering marginalized communities, promoting diversity and inclusion, and investing in targeted social programs, we will forge a more just and cohesive society that offers equal opportunities for success and fulfillment.

Achieving this transformative vision will not be without its challenges. However, our unwavering determination, strategic partnerships, and the strategic integration of technological innovations give us the confidence to turn this ambitious blueprint into a reality.

By meticulously implementing the "Project 2025 Blueprint," we will not only secure the wellbeing of our nation, but also contribute to the collective advancement of humanity. This legacy will inspire others to join us in shaping a brighter, more sustainable, and more equitable future for all.